Wibble-Wob

Grandad sat down
to eat his soup.
The table went wibble-wobble.
"One leg is too short,"
said Grandad.
"What can I do?"

3

He put a match
under the short leg.
The table still went
wibble-wobble.

He put a matchbox under it.
It still went wibble-wobble.

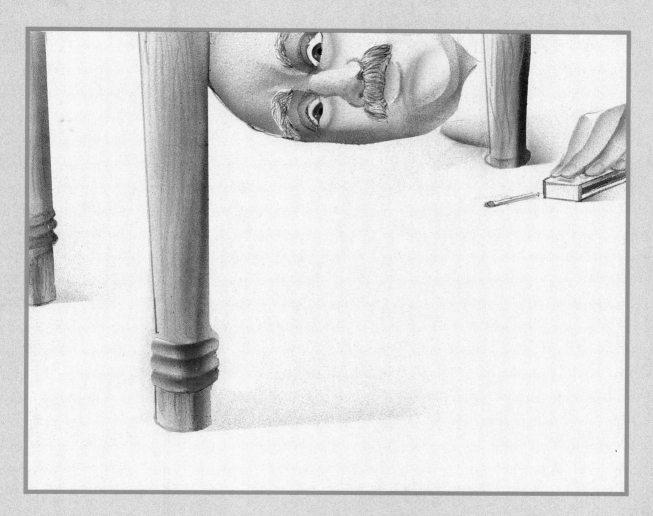

5

He put a book under it.
The table did not go wibble-wobble.

Grandad began to eat his soup.

In came Winnie.
"Hello, Grandad," she said.
"Will you read me
that story again?"

9

"Do you mean the one about the princess and the hang-glider?" said Grandad.

"Yes," said Winnie.
"I liked that story."

"I can't read it any more," said Grandad.

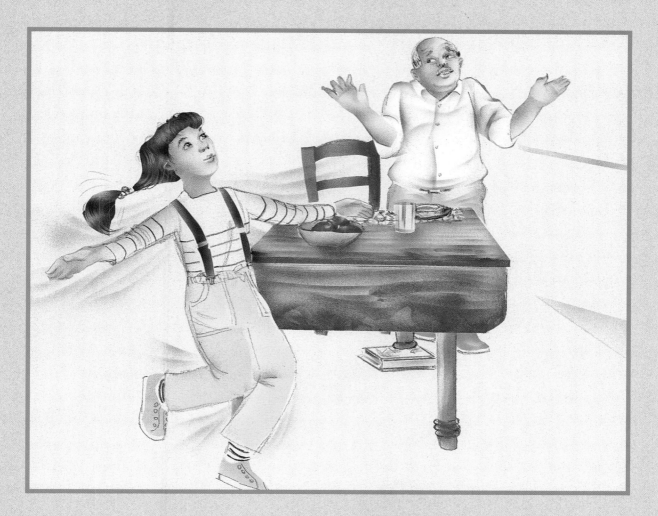

"Why not?" asked Winnie.

"The book is under
the leg of the table,"
said Grandad.

"Take it out," said Winnie.

"I can't," said Grandad.
"If I do, the table will go
wibble-wobble,
and I'll spill my soup."

"Why does the table go
wibble-wobble?" asked Winnie.

"One leg is too short,"
said Grandad.

15

"Let me see," said Winnie.
She looked at the table.

"Oh, Grandad!" she laughed.
"The other legs are all too long!"

Grandad looked, too.
"What shall I do?"
he asked.

"Get your saw,"
said Winnie.
"Cut the long legs
a little shorter."

19

So Grandad got his saw.
He cut the long legs
until they were the right length.

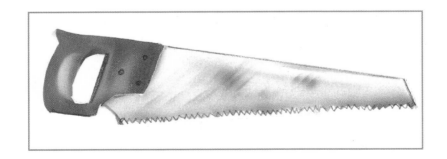

"What a good idea," he said.

"I have lots of good ideas," said Winnie.

Then she sat down to hear the story of the princess and the hang-glider.

23

And the table did not go
wibble-wobble at all.